Keepsake Letters to My Child

Lupita Wiles

Keepsake Letters to My Child

Trilogy Christian Publishers
A Wholly Owned Subsidiary of Trinity Broadcasting Network
2442 Michelle Drive
Tustin, CA 92780

For information, address Trilogy Christian Publishing

Rights Department, 2442 Michelle Drive, Tustin, Ca 92780.

Trilogy Christian Publishing/ TBN and colophon are trademarks of Trinity Broadcasting Network.

For information about special discounts for bulk purchases, please contact Trilogy Christian Publishing.

Manufactured in the United States of America

10 9 8 7 6 5 4 3 2 1

Library of Congress Cataloging-in-Publication Data is available.

ISBN: 978-1-63769-508-1

ISBN: 978-1-63769-509-8

My Child,

You are worthy.
You are worthy in Him.
Your worth comes from the Lord.

A Note from the Author:

What if our children could read our words and feel our love? At any time. That is the goal of this book. Inspirational letters serve as guiding prompts for you to write your own letter to your child.

This Book of Letters Belongs to,

_____

Dear Lord,

My heart praises you for the gift of my
humbly ask that you watch over my child
strengthen my child to your will, to becom
and the Kingdom of Heaven.

My child, may you know,

Hebrews 4:12 (KJV)

12 For the word of God is quick, and p⟨
than any twoedged sword, piercing even
der of soul and spirit, and of the joints ⟨
discerner of the thoughts and intents of ⟨

May you place His word above all
when to rest, when to work and when to
and a grateful servant of the Lord, with
and a kind and peaceful nature. Amen.

My Dear Child,

God knit you in my womb and He prepared me for you. With your birth I had a rebirth. I became a parent to you and oh, what a gift that is to me. I am filled with wonder and gratitude at the thought that you will read these letters someday and that I will be able to share my heart, with you forever in this way. I dedicate this book to you for spiritual guidance through life. May you feel my love through these letters.

Each letter is meant to serve a purpose in your life. Some will help guide you on everyday matters and some are letters for special occasions. I pray that each letter may serve its purpose in your life. As your life unfolds, I hope that you will turn to these letters to feel my love and prayers for you.

Psalms 139:13-14 (KJV)

[13] For thou hast possessed my reins: thou hast covered me in my mother's womb.

[14] I will praise thee; for I am fearfully and wonderfully made: marvellous are thy works; and that my soul knoweth right well.

You Belong to God.

Dear Child,

Our Father, He loves you. You are worthy, just because He created you. You are fearfully and wonderfully made, just the way you are. For such a precious gift as you, I give my life and yours to Jesus. I want His blessing over my soul, my spirit, and my body, so that you too, will be blessed in this world. With my surrender, I lay myself at God's feet, may He create in me, a mother worthy of you and your love.

Psalms 139:15-16 (KJV)

[15] My substance was not hid from thee, when I was made in secret, and curiously wrought in the lowest parts of the earth.

[16] Thine eyes did see my substance yet being unperfect; and in thy book all my members were written, which in continuance were fashioned, when as yet there was none of them.

I Love You.

Dear Child,

I love you with my whole being. My heart is yours, from the minute you were born. I fell in love with you. It was love at first sight. I prayed for you. My life was changed forever. Even now, thinking about your existence, in my life, I have tears rolling down my face. Tears of joy for the gift of you in my life. Tears of gratitude, because of you, I became me.

You see, the wondrous thing about having children, is that it is life transforming. Life became less about me and more about you. Raising you is the greatest joy of my life. Teaching you to know God is everything. I pray always for your peace and happiness, for your protection always, and for the strengthening of your spirit. May you know God is for you, for all the days of your life.

Proverbs 22:6 (KJV)

[6] Train up a child in the way he should go: and when he is old, he will not depart from it.

Your Worth.

Dear Child,

The world will try to pull you in many different directions. The world will also try to place so many exterior titles on you to label your worth. Remember. Your worth comes from the Lord.

Make God your center. He will help to guide you and keep you grounded. Make faith and gratitude a daily practice so that you too can feel His presence and experience the joy of fulfillment in the present. Make prayer your first language so that you are always in conversation with Him. Trust that when you take a wrong turn, He will bring you back to the right path.

Remember. Your worth comes from the Lord. You are worthy in Him.

1 John 3:1 (KJV)

[3] Behold, what manner of love the Father hath bestowed upon us, that we should be called the sons of God: therefore the world knoweth us not, because it knew him not.

Allow His Holy Spirit to Dwell in You.

Dear Child,

Invite Him daily. Ask Him to dwell in you. Welcome His presence into you and into every place with you. Some places will need God and you are the vessel. All you need to say is, "Holy Father, You are welcomed in this place. God, come." and He will. His presence will fall on you like peace. Breathe deep in the moments when you feel anxious, tense or scared. Breathe Him in and ask Him for His peace. Know that He will always come to your rescue when you call on Him. He has never let me down. He will not let you down.

Romans 15:13 (KJV)

[13] Now the God of hope fill you with all joy and peace in believing, that ye may abound in hope, through the power of the Holy Ghost.

The Lord's Will is Perfect.

Dear Child,

Ask God to align your hearts desires with His will. Whatever you ask of Him understand that His will be done. He will grant you your heart's desires only when you are working in His perfect will and are serving your purpose. This is hard. We all want so many different things, but what I have learned is that letting go and allowing God's will to take over your desires, brings far greater happiness and blessings that we could not imagine. We have many purposes as we have many seasons of growth and challenges. We think we know what we want and what is best, but truly God knows us far better than we know ourselves. He will create a life of fulfillment for you if you allow Him to have His will in your life. Acknowledge Him and He will acknowledge you.

Romans 12:1–2 (KJV)

¹² I beseech you therefore, brethren, by the mercies of God, that ye present your bodies a living sacrifice, holy, acceptable unto God, which is your reasonable service.

² And be not conformed to this world: but be ye transformed by the renewing of your mind, that ye may prove what is that good, and acceptable, and perfect, will of God.

His Sovereignty.

Dear Child,

Amid uncertainty and seasons of change or loss, remain faithful in His sovereignty. God's sovereignty covers the universe. God will make everything right in the end. Perhaps, not when you want it, but He knows when. That is the great mystery of God. His timing is best in everything. Let go. Let God do His work in you, and through you. Everything will be understood in His time. I do not have all the answers for you for everything that may happen in your life. I have but one piece of advice, take it from my own experience, believe in God. Believe in His Omnipotence, and Omniscient sovereignty. He knows what you will need during difficult times. Just ask Him. He wants to be invited into your world daily. He is your best friend and your heavenly Father.

Colossians 1:16–17 (KJV)

[16] For by him were all things created, that are in heaven, and that are in earth, visible and invisible, whether they be thrones, or dominions, or principalities, or powers: all things were created by him, and for him:

[17] And he is before all things, and by him all things consist.

God is Love.

Dear Child,

   His Love is what connects us to the rest of the world. When you pray, ask Him for guidance on matters of the heart. Pray for your future spouse. Pray for your children, your community, and the world. God needs us to pray because faith carries our prayers forward. He listens, and He works in our favor. Perhaps our prayers will not be answered because His will be done. Rest assured, always that His will is a gift that we need to recognize in our lives. His will is perfect and ours is not. What we desire may not align with His will and that is why you must pray for His will to be yours. There is freedom in not knowing all the reasons why. Have faith. It is enough that God knows why. Someday we will know the why to many of our questions.

1 John 4: 7-12 (KJV)

⁷ Beloved, let us love one another: for love is of God; and every one that loveth is born of God, and knoweth God.

⁸ He that loveth not knoweth not God; for God is love·

⁹ In this was manifested the love of God toward us, because that God sent his only begotten Son into the world, that we might live through him.

¹⁰ Herein is love, not that we loved God, but that he loved us, and sent his Son to be the propitiation for our sins.

¹¹ Beloved, if God so loved us, we ought also to love one another.

¹² No man hath seen God at any time. If we love one another, God dwelleth in us, and his love is perfected in us.

How to Live.

Dear Child,

Serve the Lord. Learn what your spiritual gift is. God created you with a spiritual gift to serve Him and others on earth. Creating experiences rather than storing up treasures for yourself will provide a life fulfilled. Learn the love languages of all those you care about so that you can love them best. Giving is the best remedy for sadness. Look for others, especially those less fortunate, to serve when your spirit is down and in the joyful giving of your heart you will lift your spirit. A giving heart is joyous in abundance. I encourage you to try your best in everything. Failures are wonderful paths to resilience and success. Allow yourself to try and fail and learn to grow from each one. Faithfulness to Jesus is the key to happiness and the gates of Heaven for you.

Colossians 3:23-24 (KJV)

23 And whatsoever ye do, do it heartily, as to the Lord, and not unto men;

24 Knowing that of the Lord ye shall receive the reward of the inheritance: for ye serve the Lord Christ.

Be Christlike.

Dear Child,

You are worthy of all the beauty that God has to offer on earth. Offer your authentic value back to the world by making it a better place. Your spiritual gifts are freely given to you and those will help you serve others.

Love. Show your heart and give love freely and unconditionally.
Grace. Show mercy and compassion always.
Kindness. Share it everywhere and with everyone.
Serve. Always with the best version of yourself.
Align. With God's purpose for your life.
Joy. Allow the Lord to dwell in you, He is joy.
Patience. Patience creates in us wisdom.
Forgiveness. Is freeing, even when not asked for it.

1 John 2:6 (KJV)
[6] He that saith he abideth in him ought himself also so to walk, even as he walked.

Be Yourself. Always.

Dear Child,

You were made perfect in the eyes of God. You are made in His image and your worthy of love. Perfection is not a quality anyone possesses. I want you to be authentically you. Those who are your people, your tribe, your friends, and your family will love you, the authentic you. You will not need to impress or change who you are to fit in. Impressing others is never a worthy goal in your life. Allow your personality to shine and dress yourself in courage, kindness, compassion and grace. God will bring all the right people to you. Always pray for others, especially your family and your friends. I am already so proud of you. I will always love you just for who you are. You are worthy just the way you are. Your worth comes from the Lord.

Ephesians 2:10 (KJV)

[10] For we are his workmanship, created in Christ Jesus unto good works, which God hath before ordained that we should walk in them.

On Your Graduation.

My Child,

I can see you now, in your cap and gown, walking on that stage and my eyes fill with tears at the sight that you are. You are beautiful, and you are filled with joy. Full of potential and confidence. Humbled by your achievement. Thank you, Heavenly Father for blessing my child all these years with opportunities to serve the world. How proud I am of you! I can burst with joy! Your efforts and your work have brought you to this day. Enjoy your achievement, you deserve it.

May this day be one that you can savor for a lifetime.

Jeremiah 29:11 (KJV)

[11] For I know the thoughts that I think toward you, saith the LORD, thoughts of peace, and not of evil, to give you an expected end.

On Your Wedding Day.

My Precious Child,

Before you go, let me hold you, as I remember holding you for the very first time in my arms. I prayed for this day. You are so beautiful. I love you and I am so proud of whom you have become. You have chosen to share your life, share your body, and share your dreams with someone you love. I delight in your happiness and am grateful for your joy. As you cleave to your spouse, ask God to go before you. Always put God first in your marriage. He is your counselor. He will guide you through marriage. This chapter brings so many new beginnings for you and I long for your marriage to be blessed.

Ephesians 5:25-30 (KJV)

[25] Husbands, love your wives, even as Christ also loved the church, and gave himself for it;

[26] That he might sanctify and cleanse it with the washing of water by the word,

[27] That he might present it to himself a glorious church, not having spot, or wrinkle, or any such thing; but that it should be holy and without blemish.

[28] So ought men to love their wives as their own bodies. He that loveth his wife loveth himself.

[29] For no man ever yet hated his own flesh; but nourisheth and cherisheth it, even as the Lord the church:

[30] For we are members of his body, of his flesh, and of his bones.

When You Become a Parent.

My Sweet Child,

What a precious moment when you hold your baby for the first time. Your whole world changes in that moment and you realize your greatest treasure here on Earth is your child. Becoming a parent, yourself is one of God's greatest gifts to us and the best opportunity to raise disciples in the truth of the Lord. Having your own child is a joy like none other but it is a responsibility to lead them into the Kingdom of God. Pray for your child, cover them with prayer day in and day out. Love your child no matter what mistakes they make for we are not here for judgment rather we are here to show God's love to all people, especially our own children. Dedicate them at an early age to God and don't worry too much about who they will become. As a healthy tree blooms fruit so too will the fruit be healthy. All you must do is model Christlike living, and they will follow your lead. Allow your children to be who they are meant to be and allow yourself as a parent to revel in their littleness. They grow so fast. Breathe their littleness daily and give yourself constant grace for parenthood is hard but it is so worth it. I love you my sweet child, and I am so proud of you and the parent that you are.

Psalm 127:3 (KJV)

[3]Lo, children are an heritage of the Lord: and the fruit of the womb is his reward.

On Days of Suffering

My Precious Child,

Gently kneel in surrender. Allow the tears to wash over you. Tears are a release for the soul and rest for the spirit. Ask the Almighty to come by your side. Even when you do not know what to say, His comfort will hold you. Whatever is hurting you, and causing you pain, lay it down at His feet. Give that pain and that suffering over to Him. Visualize yourself gently handing it over to Him. See Him taking it from you. He has it and He has you. He can help you bear the pain. He can heal your wounds and quench your need for respite. Now surrender yourself over to His comfort. Let it go. When you are ready, pray: *Father, it hurts. I am broken. I do not know what to do or what to think. I need you. Lord, please speak.*

Be still…allow yourself a few minutes to give Him space to come to you…eyes closed.

Romans 5:3 (KJV)

[3] And not only so, but we glory in tribulations also: knowing that tribulation worketh patience;

When I am Gone, I am Always with You.

Dear Child,

I will always be with you. Even now, in this very moment. I am with you. You carry me in your heart. When I am no longer phys- ically available to you, you must know how much love I continue to pour out to you. May you feel  my presence in your life always. I believe God allows our spirits to continue to flow through the Holy Spirit. Touch your heart, with your right hand, feel the beat, feel your breath slowly rising and falling. This is where you shall put your hand when you need to feel me near you. In the same way, give yourself a hug. Cross your arms. Above the elbows and below the shoulders. This is me hugging you. Do this when you need a hug from me. I will be there in that tender hug. I will live in your heart. I will wait for you in the Kingdom of Heaven with Our Heavenly Father, with arms wide open ready to receive you when your time comes.

2 Corinthians 5:8 (KJV)

[8] We are confident, I say, and would prefer to be away from the body and at home with the Lord.

CPSIA information can be obtained
at www.ICGtesting.com
Printed in the USA
BVHW051346130522
636963BV00003B/7